"Taking Control of Your Life from the Inside Out"

Eight Keys to Fulfillment on Your Job and Every Area of Your Life

"Taking Control of Your Life from the Inside Out"

Eight Keys to Fulfillment on Your Job and Every Area of Your Life

Dr. Tunishai Anne Ford

Your Own Uniqueness, Inc.
Southgate, Michigan

Taking Control of Your Life from the Inside Out.

ISBN 978-1-329-05255-0

Published by: Your Own Uniqueness, Inc. in Southgate, Michigan

Printed and bound in the United States of America by Lulu.com publishing.

CONTENTS

Dedication

This book is dedicated to you, the reader. Because you have made a decision to read this book indicates that you are a person that is serious about taking control of your life. You want to make a contribution to the world by giving it your abilities and talents. Therefore you have taken your first step and will now embark on a journey to fulfillment in every area of your life. I dedicate this book to you, the reader for you are a people of purpose and will inevitably fulfill your destiny.

Acknowledgement

First and foremost, I acknowledge my Creator for giving me the ability and desire to write this book. I have come to fully understand why we must work and know our value to the world. It doesn't matter what form of work just as long as it is done in a manner that contributes to this planet and its inhabitants.

I also acknowledge my editor and friend, Toni Coleman, whose dedication and devotion to this project has brought this book to fruition. Toni, you are a gem and are a God send. Because of your abilities, gifts and skills, this book is able to be read by the masses. I could not have done this without you.

Finally, I acknowledge my other friends and my relatives who believed in me and encouraged me. Thank you very much because I trust your judgment and you have helped me to do my best. I am inspired to keep on trying and producing other works that will be a blessing to the world.

Preface

The correlation between your work performance and your personal life has been a topic that has been in the forefront of my mind for quite some time and I believe it was my mandate to get the message out. It's understood that most employers are only concerned about productivity and making a profit, but the concern should be placed on the totality of the employee's life and the value they bring to the workplace. The concept of work is the tool that is used to build and shape our society, communities, neighborhoods and families. If work is not present, then everything we know that is tangible will cease to exist. Mankind cannot thrive if he is not constantly producing. This is the mandate for us which started way back in the beginning of time in the Garden of Eden ***(Genesis 3: 19)***. It is for this purpose that we bring value to our existence.

When work ceases to exist, it is like a dominoes affect, things become chaotic. Families break down, communities become infested with crime and deprivation, and our economy is such that we cannot properly fulfill and maintain sufficient wealth to run our nation. The problem has been said to be a lack of jobs, and that may be true to a certain extent. But the real problem is that there is a lack of people who qualify to fill the positions that are available. The lack of qualification is not just due to a lack of skill and education, but it is more contributed to a lack of the right mindset and drive. When people are dissatisfied with their lives and themselves, they are not motivated to work or do anything productive. It is difficult to concentrate on being productive when you are an emotional, psychological and physical wreck. Of course, the finances are impacted because that individual who is in a rut is not working and has no desire to work.

Taking Control of Your Life from the Inside Out is a tool that will challenge the reader to examine themselves and put forth an effort to move forward towards changing their mindset and actions. There are eight keys to instruct you, the reader, to help you assess where you are and where you want to go in your professional and personal life. The eight keys, eight denoting new beginnings, highlights the areas that are most likely to affect you from progressing, and gives strong suggestions as to how to conquer those negative areas. They will also assist you in moving forward and obtaining success by elevating to the next level which will bring fulfillment on your job and every area of your life.

I encourage you not to take this topic lightly. It is a life changing experience that you need. Success is not just about money, in fact, wealth has very little to do with money. It is about a lifestyle and a mindset and having the peace to enjoy it. When you, the reader, understand that you personally bring value to the world by your contribution of work, you will then begin to fully understand that the only way you can make a conscious contribution to the world will be by first being whole, healthy, content and happy individuals who have challenged themselves to take control of their lives from the inside out. Make the first step to adding value to the world----start with you.

Introduction

There is a correlation between success in your personal life and your job performance. Having a healthy mind, body and soul will greatly impact how you succeed in your life, including the workplace. Understand that we were created to work which is the avenue in which we discover our purpose and destiny; it is in the area of working that we find fulfillment in life and compensation for it. When we are content in our personal lives, that contentment transcends into every area of our lives, especially our jobs. What we do to make a living for ourselves often defines who we are and what we can become.

Work gives us a sense of gratification and purpose. We also make better employees and productivity for our employer is accomplished. But what if we are not content and we have challenges that hinder us from performing at our best? It will impact every area of our lives, which is seen especially on our jobs in our job performance. There is hope, but it is going to take a commitment to making some changes in our lives to fulfill this goal and it will certainly be a challenge, but not impossible

Life challenges can sometimes be overwhelming and often takes a toll on us in every area of our lives, especially in the workplace. We even find ourselves asking if we brought many of the problems we face on ourselves, or are we truly just victims of circumstances. Life is not a fair player and it is certainly not interested in letting you have the winning hand, but that's life. Although we are not always dealt a good hand, we can still end up on top and living a very fulfilling and happy life. We can dare to dream and fulfill them, and we can discover and reach our full potential and when it is all over--- give that hollow grave an empty shell.

Yes, we can take control of our lives and be the best we can be, but not without change, and not without making wise choices. Wherever you are in your life, you did not get here overnight nor did you get there without the influence of circumstance and people. It's time for us to make up our minds that we are going to be people of character and purpose. It's time to have a healthy body so that we may operate at optimum performance. It's time to have healthy nurturing relationships with others where there is mutual respect exhibited from both parties. It's time to have a meaningful sincere relationship with our Creator and allow Him to orchestrate our lives and take us to a level of perfection that we can not even phantom. Understand that He created us to fulfill a purpose to help complete His vision for the world. It is our job to find out just what part we play in God's plan. He desires that we be at our best in every area of our lives. He does not want lack in any parts of it. He is concerned about you and what concerns you, and He desires to perfect that area.

I say this because I know the plans that I have for you. This message is from God. "I have good plans for you. I don't plan to hurt you. I plan to give you hope and a good future" (Jeremiah 29: 11, ERV).

I learned that during every ordeal I have ever experienced and successfully came through, I can take control of my life and destiny by applying certain principles. True change comes from within and it starts with choices and it ends with positive and lasting results. That's right, lasting results. It's like loosing the weight and keeping it off, carrying a baby to full term and giving birth to a healthy child. No half stepping like the resolutions that you make every New Year's Day in excitement, knowing that you do not intend to keep them. It is time out for empty promises to yourself. Aren't you tired of the same humdrum life? Just never feeling satisfied, and going in the same circle over, and over again, wandering how long it will take you before you make any head-way.

It could be that you are in a relationship that you know is not going anywhere and it is not good for you. It may be a dead end job, no morale and no benefits. It could be a position in your church that you have held for years. You know God has called you to do something else, but because of your loyalty to the pastor and the church, you stay in the same position and you are dying on the inside. Maybe you are overweight and you are tired of being fat and tired of throwing your money away on these fade diets, but you do not know which diet is best for you. Therefore, you continue to eat more because you are frustrated being overweight. Does any of this sound familiar?

During some of the lowest and most difficult times in my life, I realized that I was not going to come out of it successful without change and making choices that would ensure a positive outcome. There were times when I just got quiet and asked myself ---what are you learning from all of this? Now looking back and having gone through, I realized that my success came from overcoming many of the pitfalls in my life and applying eight principles that helped me to generate growth. I want to give you these eight keys to achieve fulfillment in your professional life and every area of my life. When I began to execute these principles, I began to see change and I want to help you see changes too. The number eight denotes "New Beginnings and Total Transformation." I believe that when you apply these eight golden nuggets to every area of your life, you will begin to live and live well—starting from the inside out.

Chapter One

Key #1: Free Yourself from Toxic Relationships

We are social people; therefore, we cannot exist without interaction with someone. But oftentimes, we are not always wise in selecting who we choose to interact and form relationships with in our lifetime. Because many of us have made poor choices in forming lasting bonds, we often find ourselves in destructive situations, and failure to get out of them can prove to be detrimental. This is why I believe that the very first element to fulfillment in your life is to have a balanced and healthy relationship with others and when we do not, it is time to free ourselves from them.

Consequently, the first key to taking control of your life from the inside out is free yourself from toxic relationships This key is pivotal in experiencing success in your life, in fact, I have written a book concerning this topic, ***I Miss the Hugs, but Not the Hurts,*** which deals with coming out of toxic and co-dependent relationships. It is imperative for us to understand that relationships are the backbone of our existence and when we are not in right standing with others, it impacts us physically, mentally, and emotionally. In truth, there have been studies performed and their findings have indicated that many sicknesses and diseases have developed, such as many forms of cancers as a result of being in toxic relationships. For example, undue stress alone causes sickness in our bodies. In addition to stress are, obesity, hypertension and sleep deprivation just to name a few. All of these illnesses can be a direct result of being in a toxic relationship.

Several years ago, I was diagnosed with Hodgkin's disease and I was in the fourth and last stage of the illness. Hodgkin's disease is a form of cancer that attacks the Lymphatic system of the body. Through research and prayer, I discovered that my body was experiencing a breakdown as a result of stress and one of the stress factors was due to bad relationships in which I was harboring unforgiveness. (I will discuss this in the next chapter.) I allowed myself to get involved with the wrong men and I had no idea how much of a toll it had on my physical body and my psychological and emotional state; it was a repeated offence. I allowed myself to endure this pain over and over again. Finally, my body could not take it anymore and I became gravely ill; almost to the point of death. You can read about my trial and triumph over this ordeal in my book; ***This is a Comma in Your life, Not a Period***. Even after that ordeal, like many others, I still allowed myself to get involved in other toxic relationships. It was not until my son had to come to my rescue and I saw how disappointed he was in me that I realized all this had to truly stop for good.

We need to understand that toxic relationships not only affect us, but our loved ones as well. They too go through the physical, psychological and emotional trauma. I am proud to say that my toxic relationship sobriety has been well over ten years and I intend to keep it that way. I understand that no one wants to be alone, but it's not healthy to be miserable with the people we have in our lives. Ask yourself this question—what is it going to take that before you learn you are worthy of being loved and being happy even if you have to wait on it?

When you involve yourself with the wrong people, it is going to affect everything you do. This also means your job performance. As I mentioned previously, your job is what helps you discover purpose and fulfillment in your life, not to mention provides the means for your financial stability. When your personal life is not healthy, it will grossly impact your work performance and you will have a very unhappy boss and co-workers. Right now, some of you may be saying to yourselves, "I don't like my job and this is not what I want to do for the rest of my life". I hear you, and I know where you are coming from, but every job offers you something whether you want to admit it or not. Think about it if you did not have your present job, you may not know what you liked or disliked, also because you have your present job, you are learning new skills. Yes, that is right---you are actually learning something. It may be something as simple as learning how to close a sale or using an engraving machine. If you did not have that job, would you have obtained that knowledge staying home watching soap operas all day? Now just think about this truth if you are in a toxic relationship, you would be more miserable than you would realize. When you have a balance in your life, a not so fulfilling job does not seem so bad. You learn the skills the job has to offer and incorporate those skills into your professional repertoire. A healthy personal life helps lead you to a fulfilled professional life. Your attitude is good and you see the benefits in being right where you are for the time being. Your present job is probably preparing you for your dream job or starting your own business.

I believe you get the gist of what I am saying about coming out of toxic relationships and why I deem it to be most important for your overall being. It is understood that leaving a relationship is not easy. Easier said than done, right? If it were that easy, you probably would have left a long time ago, right? Remember this—your toxic relationship is impacting those who are truly dear to you and it's affecting your job performance. Sooner than later, it is going to affect your health and you may end up fighting an insidious disease or it can lead to death.

Allow me to share with you a story that was told by Pastor T. D. Jakes in one of his sermons. I believe you will fully understand how important it is to avoid and come out of toxic relationships. As the story was told---there was a bird watcher who was out observing different species of birds when he was lucky enough to see an eagle flying magnificently overhead. Higher and higher the bird made its way into the clouds. He watched the creature fly toward the earth and swoop up a small mammal. As the bird watcher continued to watch the incident, he realized that the animal was a weasel. The eagle flew higher and higher with his prey, when suddenly he saw that the eagle's flying pattern was interrupted. He could see the bird was in great agony. With the binoculars in his hand, he looked intently and saw the weasel gnawing at the breast of this magnificent bird until the bird could no longer stay in flight and it suddenly fell to its death. The bird watcher was amazed at this. He could not quite understand why this happened. He ponder awhile and hung his head and said to himself---"What a tragedy, this was an unnecessary death; all the eagle had to do was let go."

Many of you have weasels in your lives and they are gnawing at your heart and soul, and you continue to carry the weight of their burden when you do not have too. Like the eagle, all you have to do is let go. Why continuously allow yourself to suffer undue stress and turmoil in your life when you are completely in control of the situation. It doesn't matter whether it is a relative, a so-called friend or a lover, you can come out of that relationship and start your life over and experience a new beginning. The choice is yours.

I have been where many of you are right now and the eagle story had a profound impact on my life. I put into practice what the eagle did not realize he could do, just let go. Surely we are all more magnificent and wonderful than an eagle, but as the eagle, many people do not know that it can be as simple as just letting go and turning away from toxicity to get a new start. I have successfully overcome this pitfall and I am prepared and equipped to share some suggestions that will result in long term and permanent solutions. The following suggestions will give you the strength to get out of and avoid all together toxic relationships:

Acknowledge you are in a toxic relationship.

The first step to healing and becoming whole is acknowledging that there is an issue. You cannot solve a problem if you truly do not know you have one. Some people actually think that having drama in their lives is normal. In fact, they would be bored if there was nothing dramatic going on in their lives. Being mistreated and disrespected is what they are accustomed to and because they have never had anyone show them anything differently, it becomes an addiction; when you have spent most of your lives going from one bad relationship to another, it's like you are a magnet for misery. You have a sickness and you need help. Say it out loud---"I have a sickness and I need help". Acknowledge you are in a toxic relationship and you want out. This has to be a constant affirmation.

I want to also point out that toxicity does not discriminate. It is assumed that low income people are the only ones impacted by this plight; not true. This plight does not discriminate. Your education, economical status nor profession has little effect on being caught up in this epidemic. As long as relationships exist, and they will, toxic relationships will always be a problem that will plague our society.

Now perhaps you do not recognize that you are in a toxic relationship and you need some of the characteristics to be identified. Allow me to identify some of the major characteristics of a toxic relationship.

- Mistreatment---comes in the form of physical, mental and emotional abuse?
- Manipulation---negative persuasion to perform behavior that is uncomfortable for you.
- Unfaithfulness---he or she are with multiple sexual partners.
- Non-committal---he or she has no intention of a committed long term relationship (marriage).
- Unattached---no desire to form a relationship with the children and other family members.
- Alienation---prohibiting you from having a relationship with your friends and family members.
- Addictions---alcohol, drugs, sex, etc.

These are the most prevalent signs of a toxic relationship. If you can identify these characteristic in the relationship you are presently in, run, do not walk. Get out of this relationship. I would also strongly suggest you purchase my book, ***"I Miss the Hugs, but Not the Hurts."*** The book is about coming out of toxic and co-depend relationships. It teaches you how to be restored, recover and discover yourself after co-dependency. The book is mainly for the women, but men have gleaned from the knowledge as well.

Once you have acknowledged that you are in a toxic relationship by the characteristics I have identified above, then you must change your mindset to begin the healing process. You have to desire more out of your life and expect it, not only from yourself but also from others. How do you expect to give your employer your best performance if your life is constantly in a ball of confusion and turmoil? Unless you were on this planet by yourself, you can expect to interact with other people. My mother taught me a very profound lesson. She would tell me this all the time and drilled it into my head. She said, "You cannot pick your relatives, but thank God, you can pick your friends". To further the lesson, I say that you may not be able to help who you fall in love with, but you can certainly help who you stay in love with. Again, the choice is yours. If you want to continue to carry the weasel, then that is your choice. But you can make a wise choice and that is, trust that you deserve better in your relationships and expect it.

Trust that you deserve better in your relationships and expect it.

Look in the mirror and affirm that you desire better in your relationships and expect it. You have been doing the wrong thing for a long time. You bought the lie that toxic relationships are all that you can have in your life and there is nothing better for you. Again, it is a lie. You are a vibrant, wonderful human being who deserves to be happy and fulfilled. Let those losers stay to themselves. Yes, they will find someone to make miserable, but that is not your problem; move on. You have to see yourself doing better. Visualize a happy person who is fulfilled and thriving in your life. Expect it! Do not give into negative thoughts about your past, because they will come. Remember you have been making wrong choices for a long time. You are new to making the right ones, but you can do it. You deserve better in your relationships because you are ***WORTHY***.

You are worthy of having better, but sometimes thinking positively about ourselves is our greatest challenge. It is far easier to think negatively than it is to think positively. It's called human nature. We have to actually make an effort to think good thoughts and say positive words, especially when we don't feel or see things going right for us. Trusting that you deserve better in your relationships and expecting it has to become a daily exercise for you. You have to make it a goal like anything else you desire to achieve. Work at fulfillment in this area of your life. Expect to draw positive people into your inner circle with positive affirmations, changing the environment where you choose to meet people and last but not least—begin to work on those areas in your character and personality that contributed to bad relationships. That's right, you played a part too. Therefore, make a commitment to work on your issues that you had in your previous relationship(s).

Make a commitment to work on your issues you had in your previous relationship(s).

You will eventually meet someone else, but it is important that you work on the issues that you had in your previous relationships. Realize it takes two to tangle. The relationship was toxic because both of you were in it. I always said that likeness attracts. You attract what is in you. So if you want to 'get the one you must be the one'. You may have provoked many of the issues you faced in your previous relationships. I am not pointing the finger at you, and do not get on a guilt trip. It is important to understand that behavior is often learned and emulated.

If you are a woman, and you are reading this book, ask yourself if you are from a family of woman who attract the wrong men. Are the women in your family controlling, manipulative and needy? If you answered, "Yes" to these questions, then ask yourself if you see the same characteristics in your own life. Be honest. If the answer is "Yes", then you must understand that those are qualities that will surely contribute to toxicity. Any man that is attracted to a woman like that has serious issues too. Those qualities are not healthy for any relationship.

If you are a man and you are reading this book, and you are possessive, jealous and violent, you need help. You do not need to be in a relationship until you get that help. I often give this advice but because there are so many women who are willing to settle, the men with these problems are not allowed to get the help they need because the wrong type of woman is willing to be with him. Therefore, there is no growth and no change. As long as there are women who are attracted to men with this toxic behavior, the cycle continues.

Take time out to examine what hindered the last relationship(s). If you are truly sincere about having a better life and being a better person, work on identifying your own faults and then work on them. You deserve to be happy and fulfilled and finding a healthy wholesome person is not out of your reach. You want fulfillment in every area of your life and being with the right person should be one of them. Work on you first and good things will be drawn to you. Start by surrounding yourself with people who "celebrate you".

Surround yourself with people who "celebrate you".

It is important that we are around people who esteem us highly and make us feel important. That is a need that all mankind needs. We are social beings who need and want to be accepted. When we are celebrated by good people, it helps us feel good about ourselves and it validates our existence. We are already validated because God validated us when He created us, but He also wants us to esteem one another ***(Philippians 2: 3)***. In order to be esteemed, we must start the process. Be friendly to obtain friends and find the value in others and let them know they are appreciated. More importantly, you must understand that the door must swing both ways. You must also look for people that you celebrate and esteem highly. Who wants to be in a relationship where they esteem someone and that person does not feel the same way about you. That is a defeated feeling. I have experienced and personally heard stories from people who celebrated (esteemed) someone and their affections and admiration was not reciprocated. The person esteemed could care less about that individual. In other words, the feelings were not mutual.

Surrounding yourself with people who "celebrate you" is not something that is going to happen overnight, but it can and will happen. Remember, it is all about choices and mindsets. It starts with you. Who do you see in the mirror when you look at your reflection? Are you worth celebrating? Of course you are, but you must believe it first. First and foremost, you have to believe that you are worthy of celebrating and having good people around you to love you, counsel you and protect you. The only way you will begin to draw the right people to you is by respecting and loving yourself. Take that step.

Respect and love yourself.

Respect is not based on what is evident on the outside; it comes from the inside and then reflects on the outside. Once you understand this concept, you are well on your way to becoming the best you. Respect is not about status or position; it's about one's perception of self. If you do not see your worth, how do you expect anyone else to see it? If you want others to treat you well, start treating yourself well. Too often we give more to others hoping to make them accept us and love us, when we do not even regard ourselves with the same attention. What's wrong with that picture?

We are to love others as we love ourselves ***(Matthew 22: 39***). The greatest love of all is the love we give to the person we see in the mirror every day. When we come to respect and love ourselves, we will not allow others to hurt us and we will not hurt others. You have heard the cliché---treat others the way you want to be treated. Well, let me add another line to that cliché. Treat yourself the way you want others to treat you. Be their example and they will follow your lead.

So often I see people, especially women, subject themselves to ill treatment and it continues to be a vicious cycle from one relationship into another. Unfortunately, they are tired of the drama, but they do not know how to avoid it. They are attracted to the same type of men. Some men also have this issue; it's not exclusive to women. This cycle starts from a very young age. It is often attributed to early environment and examples shown to them by their parents. Therefore, they have lived their entire lives believing that love has to hurt and they must subject themselves to mistreatment. In order to learn to respect and love yourself, you must first re-teach yourself that respect is based on self-awareness. You must first be aware that societal values do not necessary mean that you have to reflect them on to yourself. Becoming self-aware of who you are and what value you hold for yourself and others is contingent on how you treat yourself and, of course, how you allow others to treat you. The only way you will adapt to this training will be by finding out who you are and this comes from spending time with you. That's right---take some time to be alone and get to know "YOU".

Take some time to be alone and get to know "YOU."

This could be one of the most difficult things you may have to do. How many people actually can say that they know themselves? The average person has spent most of their adult life in a relationship, whether good or bad, lacking the opportunity to get to know themselves. Sounds strange, huh, but it is true. If you asked someone to tell you about their assets, personality qualities and even their faults, they would have to pause a moment to think about it. Now I am not saying that they cannot do it, I am merely saying that they do not spend enough time thinking about who they really are.

I use to be the kind of woman that felt I had to have a man in my life; and I was not complete without one. For years, I was very depressed and all I desired was to have a relationship with a man. It consumed all of my thoughts and time. Because of this, I found myself time after time attracting and getting involved with the wrong men. As a result, my poor choices in men not only affected my personal life, but my professional life as well. I had to quickly regroup and get myself together. Soon after several blunders in my relationships, becoming self-aware and getting to know who I am became my priority. It was a challenge but when the real me began to surface, life became much sweeter. I am content being alone and I am quite focused about what I want from me and out of my life.

By no means am I telling anyone not to desire having another relationship, but I always advise people to take at least a year off from dating when they have come out of a bad relationship, because this will allow a few things to happen. Healing can begin, you become strengthened psychologically and emotionally, and you can start actually working on some personal goals without any distractions. If you notice, many of your great achievers accomplish their goals when they are alone. That's right; being alone will allow you to explore the untapped gifts and talents you possess and when you feel comfortable with "YOU", then allow someone else to share your life. Two completely unique, whole individuals make a great team.

Chapter Two

Key # 2: Forgive, Forgive Yourself and Let Go of the Past

Anger and unforgiveness are emotions that can be consuming and overwhelming to manage; they can damage a person's relationship with family, friends and colleagues. This emotional sickness will hinder every area of your life. It is important to forgive, forgive yourself and let go of the past, because it can cause discomfort, and sickness and disease. Studies have proven that harboring unforgiveness can be a major cause of serious health problems such as certain kinds of cancer, ulcers and heart disease. Studies have also shown that stress weakens the immune system for up to six hours and, therefore, can cause your body to be susceptible to illnesses such as the common cold and other viruses.

Holding on to the past will keep you from experiencing the good events that are awaiting you in the future. Unforgiveness is a major destroyer of achievement. It interferes with our ability to dream and aspire to accomplish our goals. Past hurts and situations have caused stagnation in relationships, professional aspirations, health issues, and emotional and psychological wellness. Oftentimes, there is a person or a situation that will trigger an emotional or psychological reaction that interferes with moving forward. There are many people who will never succeed in accomplishing and fulfilling their goals because they harbor unforgiveness and live in the past.

It is often difficult to let go of the past when the culprit you are dwelling on is you. Self-loathing is difficult to overcome because you are accompanied by 'you' everyday of your life. You have to live with—you. It is difficult to forgive yourself when the offence has probably set you back in life and has grossly affected others that you love. How do you let go of the past when what you have done appears to be hitting you in the face all of the time, especially if you have people around you who remind you of the offence? The following are a few solutions for forgiving, forgiving you and letting go of the past:

Admit that you are angry and/or hurting.

Admit that you are angry and/or hurting because when you can confront the negative emotion, you can begin the healing process. Bottling up your feelings will not make them go away. Confess, confront, and cry; this is a cleansing process. The pain has been with you a long time; therefore, realize it won't go away overnight. Once you begin to face the pain of your past and the object of your unforgiveness, you can begin to go forward. I do not want to make you believe that it will be an easy process, but it can be accomplished. You must take that first step to healing if you want to have healthy relationships, have a healthy mental state and be effective and productive on your job and/or career. Everything ties in together.

Try not to overreact.

Don't overreact, do this by stepping back from the situation and ask yourself, "Is this situation as bad as I am making it out to be?" We are our own worst enemies, when it comes down to escalating emotionally, especially we women.

Women have a tendency to exaggerate things when experiencing hurts. So, we hold on to emotions longer than it's necessary. This is one of the reasons why women have a hard time moving on when they get out of a bad relationship. They compensate for the loss by finding someone just like the one that hurt them because they do not know how to just let go! When you are trying to let go of the past and experience forgiveness, you must learn to keep things in their proper perspective. Don't overreact and try to minimize the problem by understanding one thing---this too will pass. It is your choice as to how long you want to continue to experience the pain.

Think on good things.

Now this is where you get to really using that gray matter we call a brain. Concentrate on something positive instead of what is irritating you. I know---again easier said than done, right? As I stated previously, it is up to you as to how long you stay in pain. The process of healing and growth can start with your confession and what you think about on a regular basis. Whatever a man/woman thinks of themselves that is who they are ***(Proverbs 23: 7).***

If your thoughts are self-destructing, then you will know the outcome. On the other hand if your thoughts are positive and reassuring, then you can predict the outcome of those thoughts. Remember, things are thoughts and thoughts are things. You deserve to be happy. Stop waddling in self-pity. You have been in that place too long. Give it a try---think on good things. Maybe you desire to lose weight. Start visualizing yourself in that smaller size dress or suit. Your goal may be to get a promotion on your job; begin to see yourself doing the job and work on it. Maybe you want to do some home improvement—day dream about that beautiful home that you are going to create. Its possible to feel good about life when you think on good things.

Identify the source of your anger and confront it.

If the actions or works of another person is the source of your anger, try to talk with that person directly in a peaceful and productive manner. This is what I practiced and it worked. When I was diagnosed with stage four cancer in January of 1998, I was devastated and I was frightened that I would succumb to the illness. I realized that my body attacked me because I was dealing with unforgiveness and anger. There were people in my past and present who hurt me and instead of me letting it go and doing what I am advising you to do, I became ill. I truly believe that I opened the door for cancer to come upon me. I was angry for a long time and I did not know how to let it go. I believe that God spoke to me in that still quiet voice and gave me the solution. Identify the source of your anger and unforgiveness and confront it.

How did I do it? Well, let me tell you exactly what I did. If I could contact the people whom I believed offended me, I phoned them and told them how I felt and I verbally forgave them. Also, I asked them to forgive me for harboring unforgiveness. The people who I could not connect with, I prayed and admitted that I was angry with them and asked for forgiveness. It was by faith that I forgave them.

Confront your hurt and anger if you can. You may feel uncomfortable with the idea of telling that person that they hurt you, but you will be surprised—they may be willing to face you and apologize. Those magic words—"I'm sorry" bring healing and have often constructed new beginnings.

Forgive the situation.

What does it mean to forgive the situation, you may ask? Remember, previously, I mentioned that sometimes we experience triggers that bring back memories, or you can call them flash backs. You experience something that wakes up that hurtful place that you are trying to forget. It could be a word, a scent, a building or other objects that make you think about that bad experience. You have gotten past the individual that hurt you, but events or objects trigger the hurt that you faced. I know that many of you who are reading this can relate to what I am saying. It may be that you will not allow yourself to celebrate a particular day because it brings back bad memories. It could be that you stay away from certain colors because you are convinced that they bring bad luck. Many of you have missed out on opportunities, because you could not get pass a situation.

You feel stuck in a rut, but again it is not impossible to overcome this place. Realize that each day holds something new. Anticipate good things coming to you and begin to visualize it. Forgive the situation by acknowledging that the past can no longer hurt you. Yesterday is gone and today is brand new. Don't worry about tomorrow because you haven't gotten there yet, but its okay to look forward to seeing it. It is your life and it is up to you to choose to look forward to the future or be stagnated in the past. If forgiving the situation will set you free, what are you waiting for?

Seek out professional counseling.

Sometimes we need that extra support in order to get through our issues and that's okay. In fact, I strongly suggest that everyone, at some point in their lives, seek out professional counseling. Now the manner in which you receive it is up to you. But let me give you this bit of advice;

do not allow your emotions and psychological state to get out of hand. It does not make you a weak person if you have to talk to someone who can bring a different perspective to the situation. On the contrary, by seeking out professional counseling, it proves that you are a mature individual that realizes you cannot overcome these problems alone. Depending on what you believe and how much counseling you need, just going to a social worker who specializes in counseling may be the only person you may have to see. If you are a member of a church, I would strongly suggest that you go to your pastor or a counselor who may be on staff at the church. If your problem is much more intense, then I suggest that you go and see a psychologist. Consider this, professional help is just there to give you guidance and help you see things differently. You are not a freak or a looser because you seek out help. You want to experience a better life; and oftentimes by getting help, you can come to realize that dream.

Chapter Three

Key # 3: Put Yourself in a Position for Change to take Place—Realize your Potential

Sometimes we must literally remove ourselves from situations and/or people who hinder us from being our best. This can be a life changing decision, but if you cannot pick up and move, then the change has to start within. This can happen by changing the geographical location of your attitude. Start saying affirmations that declare what you want changed in your life. As I stated, everyone cannot afford to move out the state or country to embrace a new beginning. If that were the case, many states would look like a ghost town. In fact, I would personally lead the crusade to leaving to go somewhere else. I would call it "The Somewhere Else Campaign". Since this is never going to happen, let's see if there are other alternatives to positioning change for healing to take place. It's not just about healing, but it is also about restoration and building a new foundation for a much better life.

As a reminder, this book is supposed to help you move forward and experience fulfillment in every area of your life. The objective is to create more productive, highly motivated people who desire to excel in every area of their lives, especially on their jobs. But first things first, right? We have to remove the garbage and focus on what ails us before we can give someone else our best. We have to concentrate on being the best for ourselves before we can be the best for others even if it is in the work environment.

Many employers may not care about the personal life and overall well-being of their employees, but they should. At the end of the day if there are healthy psychological, emotional and physical employees on the payroll, the employers will see the results they are looking for in their company's overall performance. Now I understand that Rome was not built in a day, and I am not predicting that this will all happen overnight, but it will happen. If change is what is necessary to ensure success, then we must initiate the steps it takes to achieve it.

Getting rid of that "stinking thinking".

The bestselling book called *"The Secret"* won critical acclaim for introducing a phenomenon called the "Law of Attraction." The law of attraction simply suggests that whatever you dwell on the most will be drawn to you. In addition, whatever you are thinking can affect the words that come out of your mouth, and the outcome of your situation. Your thoughts and words have power ***(Proverbs 18: 21).*** You have what you say. Make it a habit to speak what you want, not what you do not have. Begin to visual a healthy, whole, vibrant person who is successful, happy and fulfilled in every area of your live. Do not allow yourself to drown in self-pity and depression. It's understandable that you will experience some lows in your life, but don't stay there.

When I begin to feel off centered and sorry for myself, I realize my thinking is all wrong, I read a book entitled, *"How Forcible Are Right Words?"* I have read this powerful book several times. In fact, it is the only book I have ever read more than two times. This just goes to show you that even I do not have it all together all the time. I need to watch myself too. It is a challenge to stay encouraged when you are disappointed, but when I feel that way; I choose to focus on the bigger picture---where I am trying to go in my life.

We are always going to have bad things happen to us, and these bad things will sometimes involve people that we least expected to hurt us. This is a part of life; it's inevitable. How we handle it and go through the ordeal is what makes or breaks us. If we are going to put ourselves in a position for healing and change to take place, we must change our point of view. How do you view the outcome? What can we do to create the life we have always desired? Start with your thoughts and your words. The law of attraction is not new, in fact, it has been here forever—since the beginning of time. We can find the principle written out in the most read book in the world---the bible. Get rid of that "stinking' thinking'" and call those things that are not in your life as though they are ***(Romans 4: 17)***. Speak your change into existence. Begin with positive affirmations, prayer, meditation, and reading spiritual and motivational literature; this will be a good place to start.

Identify the enemies that hinder you from achieving your goal.

There are many areas that hinder us from moving forward and I wanted to identify many of the most prevalent ones. It is not the intention of this chapter to condemn anyone, but I believe that we must identify these problems and stop living in denial before we can truly begin to move forward.

There are twelve "potential thieves," as I would call them that I would like to identify and expound upon. These twelve "potential thieves" are the most common hindrances that prevent us from succeeding in our personal and professional lives. In order to excel, we must not allow these following hindrances to prevail any longer:

1. *Immorality*---Immoral behavior is a potential thief because it dictates to your moral judgment. When you deliberately allow yourself to partake of immoral behavior, it is inevitable that it will lead to destruction and failure. Participating in immoral behavior oftentimes lead to death. Example—promiscuity, adultery, addictions such as alcoholism, drugs and pornography.

2. *Poor Choices*---Failure to think with your mind and allowing your emotions to dictate the outcome of a situation. Many people fail to realize their potential because they spend most of their time getting out of the messes they placed themselves in. Ninety-eight percent of the problems we have in life are because we fail to "Think". We are immature in our sense of reasoning.

3. *Fear*---The opposite of faith, action, and persistence. Dwelling on what will go wrong instead of what will go right. It is a stagnation trigger to stop you from achieving and living your dreams.

4. *Discouragement*---The inability to continue to hope because events do not happen in the time frame in which we prefer. Staying focused is difficult when we put a time frame on something that we may have little or no control of.

5. *Procrastination*---Delaying an action that is necessary to realize a particular event. Procrastination is often a result of fear. Because we do not have faith, action and persistence operating, we cannot see a positive outcome.

6. *Past failures*---The inability to take risk in the present because of the failure of the past. Past failures should be looked at as another opportunity to succeed. Take the risk.

7. *The opinion of others*---The opinion and criticism of others can cause us to abandon our ideals and dreams. Looking for approval of others is a major destroyer of maximizing our potential especially if these people hold a certain influential place in our lives.

8. *Distraction*----One of the major principal enemies of maximizing your potential. When we allow anything and everything to hinder us from staying focused and on point, we are hindered from achieving our goals. Anything that doesn't help our progress hinders it.

9. *Fear of success*---Being afraid to succeed causes people to sabotage their own achievements, thus, slowing down or aborting all together their success. This is my motto—"I may be afraid of success, but I would not have it any other way. I must succeed and that settles it for me."

10. *A wrong environment*---"Bad company corrupts good character." No matter how good your intentions may be if you associate with bad

company, it is inevitable that you will think and act as they do. You will not change them, they will change you.

11. *Comparison*---Comparing your abilities and skills with others will give a false sense of self. It prevents you from becoming all that you can be. It's like looking at someone else's paper when you are taking a test. It's not your work, therefore it's not you.

12. *Societal pressures*---Pressures from society's standards and expectations. If the people we associate with in a particular setting make judgments based on who we are; age, race, education, etc., this may pressure you to relinquish a dream because they do not believe you can achieve it.

Work on having financial stability.

Prioritize your spending and work on building financial stability. It is never too late to start planning for your financial future. In fact, something as simple as having a saving account can make a difference in your financial status. Many urban employees, especially in the African-American community do not have a financial plan. No money put away for rainy days, retirement or for their children. Most of them just live from paycheck to paycheck. This is not an attack on African-Americans; it is merely an observation that I want to use to illustrate the seriousness of this matter. Enough said, but it is very important to start on building financial stability if you are going to change your life and realize potential.

Money is a very necessary commodity for having a fulfilled and successful life. It is not just enough to make it and spend it on things. I personally know people who have worked all of their adult lives and they have absolutely nothing to show for it. This is extremely sad and we want to know why our economy is in such a depressed state. It is a lack of knowledge and a lack of interest. Because the average person does not truly understand the value of money and wealth building, they cannot engage in wise spending and investing.

Having financial stability is very pertinent to realizing your potential. It is one of the top major factors to dream building, and walking in your divine purpose. I would like to give you an illustration. A few years ago, I wanted to publish two books and I found a company that could help me realize my dream; they help you to self-publish, market and publicize your books. Now, of course, I had to pay them. The cost was over three-thousand dollars and I am thankful that I had the money to pay for the cost. I got a great deal; they were running a special to publish two books for the price of one. In the summer of 2008, I published two books, ***"I Miss the Hugs, but Not the Hurts***", and ***"This is a Comma in Your Life, Not a Period"***. I believe my point is quite obvious—if I did not have the money at that time, I could not have published my two books.

Whatever your dream may be, you must have finances to achieve it, unless you have a great business plan and someone else invests in your dream. Even then, you will have to show that your dream is worth the investment so that there will be financial gain on both ends. Remember, money is the answer to all things and if you are going to realize your potential, you must have financial stability as your partner; such a partnership will bring great reward. If you truly intend to change your life and fulfill your destiny, you must take the necessary steps to achieve this goal. Here are factors that will enhance your ability to achieve financial stability:

1. *Pay yourself first.* Make a commitment to take a portion of your paycheck, ten percent is a good place to start, and do not touch it unless it is for an emergency. You should have money in a separate bank account for emergencies. The ten percent that you put away for savings is not dispensable. If you are saying to yourself right now that you do not have it, I can challenge that.

   Money that you spend on items you do not need, such as unnecessary clothing items, fast food, gambling, cigarettes, alcohol, vending machines, eating out every weekend, etc., that is money you can pay yourself. Most of the items I mentioned are things you can live without. Instead of going out to lunch, take a lunch to work; its much healthier and economical. Stop putting your money in those unhealthy vendor machines where they sell those sugary beverages and sugary and salty snacks; that is money you can save. I bet if you gave up smoking, you would have a lot of money to put into a savings account. Wouldn't you? My point exactly---when there is a will, there is a way.

2. *Save your money in a financial institution such as a bank or a credit union.* Credit unions are known to give you more for your money. I suggest you look into saving there first. It is also much easier to get a loan with a lower interest rate. Plus, financial institutions will also have investment

plans to help you grow your money. The financial planners are free; that's a perk right there.

Financial institutions have several options that will meet your needs and your money will be accumulating interest. Don't follow the example that many of your grandparents did and save your money in a drawer or an old sock. If they would have just placed their money in a financial institution, they would have ended up with hundreds of thousands of dollars just from the interest alone. This is a true statement. Many older people did not believe in banks and they saved up several thousands of dollars. If they would have banked it, the interest alone would have given them a substantial amount for their savings and retirement.

3. *Sit down with a financial planner.* Yes, I touched on this point in the previous paragraph, but now I would like to expound upon this factor. Everyone should go to a professional to discuss which financial plan of action is right for you. Again, the average person does not understand how money works or better yet, how to make money work for them. A financial planner not only tells you how to invest it, but will also look at some short term and long term goals for you in order to help achieve the goal you may have right now or in the near future.

   A bank is a good place to start because if your money is with them, they are going to do everything in their power to keep your money with them. The other perk is that it is free. If you trust your bank, then you can build a rapport with that person who will be looking out for your best interest. Because I am not an expert in this area, I will not be giving out investment and savings advice; see the experts.

4. *Another important factor for building financial stability is having medical and life insurance.* I know that you do not want to talk about it, but having it in place is good. Having medical insurance is important because if you need to see a doctor or have to go to emergency, it will cost you far less than paying the entire medical bill. I know what you are thinking---I can't afford it. You cannot afford not to have it. Think about it. If you have to see a doctor, your insurance will pick up most of the cost and you will receive the best care rather than if you did not have it. If you do not have medical insurance, all of the expense comes from your pocket. If you have an ongoing condition that requires you ongoing medical treatments, this can wipe out your entire savings and/or investment accounts. Even if you have out of pocket expenses, at some point, the insurance will pay one hundred percent. You should have yearly check-ups, mammograms, and other yearly required procedures to ensure good health. Not having medical insurance can deplete you of your efforts to build wealth. There are many plans. Again, sit down with a professional and get advice about what is best for you.

   Having life insurance is important too if you are going to be a wealthy conscious responsible individual. Many Americans do not have life insurance, especially African—Americans. I am not trying to pick on them, but just to make a point that this factor is impacting many families just because they will not take the time to obtain a policy. Not only will an insurance policy assist with final expenses, it can also leave a financial legacy for your loved ones. In addition, you do not want to place a financial burden on your family. That is cruel and extremely irresponsible.

Recently I lost a very dear family member who was in her late seventies. She was ill, but she died unexpectedly. She did not have life insurance; she was financially irresponsible. It was an embarrassment for the family because we had to ask family members and close friends to help out with her arrangements. We also asked for assistance from the State of Michigan. We could not even bury her. The question that I asked was "How could you have lived this long and not have a policy?" There are many people who do not consider their loved ones. One day everyone is going to have to cross that road. Be responsible and get a life insurance policy. Make the choice to do the right thing---be insured.

5. *Invest.* One of the best opportunities to have financial stability and build wealth is to own property. It can be having your own personal residence or buying property to sell. There are countless stories of how people became millionaires through real-estate. Wealth in real-estate can come by being a contractor/builder, buying up property and flipping it, selling real-estate or just being a home owner and taking advantage of the many perks from owning a house. Don't throw your money away by leasing property. Look who is making the money? The landlord you are paying. There are numerous books on real-estate and wealth building. If this is something that you think

you have a knack for then do it. Again, I cannot talk fluidly about the subject because this is not my forte', but I know that real-estate is quite lucrative with very few regrets.

Now if investing in property is not something you choose to do, there are other ways to invest. Again, speaking to a financial adviser is wise because they can lead you to the professionals that can assist you in making wise decisions about investing. The bottom line is this---make your money work for you. Having money outside of a regular savings is the goal. You want to build wealth and the way to do that is to have lucrative investments. Make sure you talk to the experts. You can make major mistakes and lose a lot of money if you do not know what you are doing. Best advise—stay away from those get rich quick schemes. If it sounds too good to be true, then it probably is too good to be true.

6. *Be a giver*. This is my last advice for obtaining financial stability. Giving is a spiritual principle that comes with results ***(Luke 6: 38).*** When you have an open hand, you set yourself up to be not only on the giving end, but also on the receiving end. When you give of your time, talents and substance (money), you open up a gateway to receive many blessings. When you give bountifully you will never go without. Your needs will always be met. You may not know how they are coming, but they are coming. Not only does giving insure blessing and provision for you, but it covers your family and future descendants as well. If you are experiencing a financial drought, find an opportunity to sow a seed (give). It can be an organization (church or ministry), a charity, or

even an individual who may have a need. Watch windows of blessings come your way. It may come in many forms; a promotion, a new job, food, shelter, opportunities for advancement in your life, healing and of course the obvious---money. Giving opens up an arena you cannot even begin to fathom. If you want to see your situation change, begin to give your way out of your plight.

Seek out people who can help you see your situation in a positive manner.

If your vision is clouded, then you may need another set of eyes to see things clearly. When life dishes out lemons, you are going to need someone around you who knows how to make a lemon meringue pie. Being alone is what we automatically want to do when we are in a bad space. We often think that's best because we feel no one will understand and no one really cares anyway. Because this is how many people handle their issues, healing takes longer to come to fruition. Believe it or not if an effort is made, you can probably find someone who would be more than willing to give you a listening ear and give you good advice. They can often help you see things from a different perspective too.

I had a friend that was always able to help me see that what I was going through was never that bad. She had a way of helping me see situations differently. I would start off feeling depressed and hopeless and when I finished talking to her, I felt like everything was going to be alright, and most of the time everything did turn out to be alright.

The objective is not to stay in that place of hurt and defeat. Even if it takes going to more than one person to achieve the end result that you need, do it. Never make a life changing choice by yourself, especially if that choice is made when you are hurting. The experience will be like running into a brick wall. You will more than likely cause more damage than good. Words to the wise---there is safety from good counsel. It is wise to seek out help from someone who has been there and done that, and has successfully come out of the ordeal with good results; the key words are successfully with good results. There are people who may have experienced what you are going through, but they are not necessarily the right person to give you advice. They may have come through the ordeal, but they are bitter and angry from it. STAY AWAY FROM THEM.

A place of change comes from making a choice that this is the outcome you want to achieve. No matter what it takes, you want to get to a place where you can grow and flourish. Your success comes from being a better person overall. Begin by changing your thoughts and your words. Think on good things and begin visualizing yourself living that life. Anyone who is successful will tell you it was not easy. You see the end result, and the finished product, but they will tell you that there were many nights of tears and days of despair. They may have wanted to throw in the towel, in fact, some of them did a few times, but they got back into the game. Surround yourself with people who are positive and their lives reflect what you desire to be. They know where you are because they have been in that same place. If they are good people, be assured that they will be more than willing to share how they came through their darkest times and encourage you to do the same. Also, don't forget to work on obtaining financial stability. Money is the answer to all things. Remember the cliché if you want to get different results, start doing something different. Above all, know and understand that all things are possible if you believe. The battle is not given to the strong, but the one who endures to the end.

Chapter Four

Key # 4: Get Rid of the Bad Rituals and Habits

When you work for a living, it is very easy to form bad habits and rituals because you are trying to maintain a strenuous schedule. These habits and rituals can greatly affect our health and wellness, thus, causing a rift in our job performance. Being willing to take a look at some of these habits and rituals and changing some of them to alleviate stress and improve the quality of your life is the objective of this chapter. If you want to perform at your optimum capacity on your job, you must incorporate good habits into your lifestyle that will ensure you are performing at your best. These changes may appear to be drastic, but in the long run they will prove to be a life saver.

When I was in the workforce, I was employed with Detroit Public Schools and I taught adult education. My duties were to prepare adult students for their GED and also teach employability skills. I worked every day except Fridays from 9:00am to 9:00pm. To even complicate matters, I had a teenage son that was very much involved in sports and I supported him by attending his games as often as possible. When I was not going back and forth to his games, I had a dog that I had to rush home to care for. As I reflect back on those days, I wonder how I was able to maintain this schedule and keep my sanity. This went on for years. When my assignment changed, I had to drive all the way from one site to another that was on the other side of town. It was not only a lot of wear and tear on my vehicle, but it was also a lot of wear and tear on my physical body. You could just imagine the kind of foods I ate and the lack of exercise I got. On the weekends, all I wanted to do was rest and on occasion, go out to a movie and dinner with a friend.

After about four years of working like that, I became gravely ill. I was diagnosed with Hodgkin's disease. I was in the fourth and last stage of the illness. I had a tumor in my chest and one on my spine. It was for many months that I was ill before I even knew I was sick. I had a difficult time doing my job because I was in excruciating pain. I ended up having to leave my job for almost a year. I am taking out the time to share this with you to make you aware of just how important it is to maintain good health. I thought I was healthy, but I shared with you, previously, I had some emotional and psychological issues that I was dealing with that eventually spilled over into affecting my physical health; in addition, I know I was not eating right either.

I would like to share with you three areas that most of us get caught up with that causes us to perform inefficiently in our personal lives as well as on the job. Of course there are several more, but the three areas I am going to expound upon are the ones that I believe are causing the most hindrance in our personal and professional lives. Again, I am not a specialist in these areas, but I have enough personal experiences and references to understand that these behaviors can prove to be detrimental to our overall well-being.

- **Insufficient rest**—going to bed too early or too late interferes with you being alert and performing at your physical and psychological best. Studies have been done to prove that sleep deprivation can prove to be hazardous in many ways. Here are ten of the major hazardous things that can happen as a result of having insufficient rest, better known as sleep deprivation:

1. *Public Safety hazard.* Sleep deprivation is a public safety hazard. The National Highway Traffic Safety Administration estimates that fatigue is the cause in 100,000 auto crashes and 1,550 crash—related deaths in the U.S. The problem is greatest among people under 25 years old.

2. *Affects ability to think and learn.* When you are deprived of sleep, it does not allow the brain to operate at optimum capacity, therefore interfering with mental alertness.

3. *Leads to serious health problems.* Chronic sleep loss can put you at risk for the following illness: Heart Disease, Heart Attacks, Heart failure, Irregular heartbeat, High blood pressure, Stroke, Diabetes, and certain types of cancer.

4. *Lowers your libido (sex drive) and interest in sex.* Lack of sleep can lead to low energy, fatigue, and sleepiness which may affect libido and/or decrease interest in sex. The combination of low energy and increased tension caused by lack of sleep (referred to as "tense tiredness") can also lead to sexual dysfunction.

5. *Contributes to the symptoms of depression.* Insomnia has the strongest link to depression.

People who were diagnosed with depression or anxiety were more likely to sleep less than six hours at night.

6. *Lack of sleep ages you.* A lack of sleep is definitely a bad cosmetologist, especially for the ladies who want to maintain that youthful appearance. It causes skin to look aged, puffy eyes, fine lines and dark circles---enough said.

7. *Lack of sleep affects your memory.* Lack of sleep impairs a person's ability to focus and learn efficiently. Sleep is necessary to consolidate a memory (make it stick) so that it can be recalled in the future.

8. *Weight gain.* A lack of sleep increases hunger and appetite which causes weight gain and can ultimately lead to obesity. It stimulates craving for high-fat, high carbohydrate foods.

9. *Increases risk of death.* Sleep of six hours or less on a consistent basis can double the risk of death from all causes, in particular cardiovascular disease.

10. *Impairs judgment, especially about sleep.* If you work in a profession where it is important to be able to judge your level of functioning, it becomes a problem because people with sleep deprivation often feel they have adapted to not getting enough sleep.

Special Note---The biggest culprits of sleep deprivation are electronic devices such as cell phone, tablets, lab tops, land lines, radios and television. If you want to get a good night's sleep, make sure that you are not allowing these items to be a distraction.

- **Procrastination**---Putting things off until the last minute causes unwanted stress. Unfortunately, this behavior has become the norm for many people. It is a very unproductive lifestyle which greatly impacts the workplace as well as ones personal life. As I mentioned in the previous chapter, procrastination is a destroyer of reaching your full potential. It has become a habit that most people wear as a blind spot. It is allowed to go on for so long that when it is too late to do something about a certain situation; you do not recognize that procrastination was the culprit.

  In their personal lives, they bring much frustration to their friends and family members because everyone knows they are going to be late, and they can develop a reputation for being unreliable. They do everything at the last minute which causes them undue stress. Sadly enough, they do not even recognize that a drastic change is necessary because they have been exhibiting this behavior for most of their lives.

- **Eating too many complex carbohydrates and sugary foods**--- One of the worst habits many people have is eating the wrong types of food. I am sure that most of you have heard the old cliché, "You are what you eat". This is truly a fact. You are what you eat, and what you do not eat. Poor eating habits plague American people more than any other country. Can you guess why? Yes, you've guessed it—we have access to more food and that also means access to all the wrong foods as well. On every other corner, especially in the suburbs, you see more fast food restaurants. Also, they have restaurants that serve extremely large portions.

Did you know that most foreigners do not have a weight issue until they come to this country? They do not eat like this in any other country. We are bombarded with food. Every time you turn on the TV, every other commercial is about food, especially at night when you are suppose to be getting ready for bed. Instead, you see a commercial that suggests that you super-size a burger and fries or pile up a lot of processed meat on a six-inch piece of bread and call it eating fresh.

You can call it a habit, ritual or lifestyle, but it has to stop. Our poor eating habits are killing us, and if we want to achieve our personal and professional goals, then we must begin to change our attitude towards food. We can start with eliminating the bad carbohydrates and sugars. This will not be an easy feat because the average person eats a lot of processed food, example foods in boxes, cans and packages—non frozen. This is certainly true for the single parent homes and homes where both parents work. Also, men and women who are single tend to eat a lot of processed foods only because it is convenient. Most of us do not intend to destroy our bodies and jeopardize our health, but it happens unconsciously.

The food manufacturers do not help the matter either. Most foods, unless they are whole foods (food that have one ingredient) have some sugar and are probably bad carbohydrates. Of course, some processed foods are worse than others. Sugary foods such as cakes, pies, donuts, etc are not good for anything, but the tongue's pallet. FYI— did you know that sugar is more addictive and deadlier than "Crack Cocaine"? It has no nutritional value and consuming it is the leading cause for weight gain and obesity. It is also a factor of inflammation and arthritis. There are other illness and diseases that sugar contributes to and they are Alzheimer's, cancer, obesity, depressed immune system, mood swings, increase risk of heart attacks, premature aging, kidney stones, and osteoporosis; the list goes on but these are the more prevalent illnesses I found based on my research.

Complex carbohydrates are not good for you because they are often high in sugar and salt. The bad carbohydrates, such as sweets, breads, and food in a box, raises blood sugar and increase chances of weight gain too. It also increases chances of high blood pressure, certain cancers and other insidious diseases. The food in this category leads to being sluggish during the day. You know what I mean. Remember how you feel at lunch time after you have gone to McDonald's to get that Big Mac and an order of fries and don't forget the diet coke; within a few minutes after consuming your food, you feel sluggish and ready to take a nap. That definably will not go over good with the boss if he or she catches you napping because you got drunk on carbs.

After eating like this for years, your body will tell it all. There are also people who are thin but they are still impacted by bad carbs as well. Remember what I stated earlier---"You are what you eat", eventually you will begin to see and feel the effects eating the bad stuff will have on you.

If you are going to be effective on your job and want to live a happy, healthy and fulfilled long life, do those two things. Get rid of the sugar in your diet and stay away from processed food. Eat right, feel right. You only have one body and there is no trading it in for a new one. This is it; take care of it. Your

> body is a gift from God, and He expects that it should last you a lifetime. Just like an old car that was well cared for even after one hundred thousand miles, it can still drive like a new car. We are going to be held accountable for how we treat or mistreat our bodies. But know one thing; it is not too late to start. Make up your mind that you want every area of your life to reflect success. Your boss should be able to get the best performance from you, but you cannot give it to him if you are always tired and in poor health. You have people who depend on you---family members and friends. Make the choice to take responsibility for your health by consciously eating the right foods and eliminating the wrong ones; I know you can do it.

Presently, I only mentioned three areas that hinder our performance on our jobs and affect our personal lives, but of course, there are many more. By working on these three areas I expounded upon, you will begin to see drastic changes in your life. Again, it is all about choices and what you want to achieve out of your life and what you want to contribute to others. Taking care of your body and being a good steward over one of the most important commodities that you have—time, will afford you an opportunity to reverse the negative lifestyle that many of you have become accustomed too. There should be a paradigm shift in your life and ridding yourself of bad habits and rituals will help you perform at your optimum best. We all have a responsibility to make an effort to live our best life now, right now and achieve our goals. In order to do that, we must throw out the old and embrace what we want to become.

Chapter Five

Key # 5: "Accept Who You are Before You Become What You Can Be"

Self-criticism should not be destructive, but constructive and realistic. Looking at the person in the mirror will help maintain a positive outlook toward ourselves and others. Do not allow yourself to get into comparing your qualities, abilities and work performance to others. Remember you are unique. There is no one else like you and your work performance and abilities will be different which is a good quality. It is your uniqueness that you bring to the table. Before we can uncover the intended qualities we wish to display, we have to be willing to accept who we are and examine the areas that we must work on improving and perfecting. Remember we are all a work in progress, but eventually with persistence and hard work, we will get there. I personally believe that a person can become self-actualized, which is someone who is walking in their divine purpose, utilizing their gifts and abilities to the fullest and using them to be a service to mankind. But before we can achieve the ultimate goal, there are certain actions that must come into play. Let's examine a few areas that can help us become the persons that we ultimately desire to be.

Work on improving your character and personality.

You always want to be a pleasant person to work with and be around. Often times, we may not think that who we portray on the outside reflects who we are on the inside. Everyone should do an assessment of themselves and ask this question, "Who am I?" Okay, a big red flag just went up. Most of you are saying right now---I know who I am. Now remember I am not asking you to say what you like and what your abilities are, I want you to think about the qualities that make you unique; your character, and your personality type. It is evident that most people may not give this question consideration because of the ugly things that are happening all over the world. If people were truly looking at themselves for who they truly are, they would be compelled to change because they would realize that the person in the mirror needs to gravely improve.

It's a fact, that most people are hung up on that which is tangible—their image, their possessions, status, and money. They feel that if they have it going on in those areas that they have arrived, and little to nothing else really matters. An individual who is looking to achieve the goal of becoming who they desire to be, must realize who and where they are in their lives and work on building from there. There is nothing worse than having a co-worker or a boss whose personality make them difficult to work with. As you are reading this, you are probably thinking about some of those people that you have worked with or are presently working with that make life miserable for you. You regret getting out of bed and going to work.

Now this brings me to my point—there is no valid reason for people to behave in a manner that warrants making others unhappy. People who act like this in the workplace are people who do not choose to be people of character. For whatever reason, they thrive on being unkind, belligerent, and controlling—just to name a few negative character traits. Maybe something happened to them and they are holding on to a past bad experience. Maybe they were unable to let go of or forgive a person or situation that keeps them engulfed in the actions that they portray. No one has the right to be cruel and mistreat people, especially in the workplace; that is called bullying, but it goes on all the time. Usually, when you see someone display that behavior, they are crying out for help and they are letting the world know that some things are out of sync in their lives and they are not content or happy. For others, it may be a learned behavior based on their environment and social values.

But enough about the other guy, what about you? Do you have character and personality flaws that need to be worked on? Did I just describe you in the previous paragraph? I hope not. If you are going to bring value to your job and personal life, you must first strive to work on your own character and personality and purpose to put your best foot forward. If you want others to respond positively to you, then you must display a character that is worthy of that positive reaction. My mother always told me as a child, pretty is—pretty does. In others words, when we act attractive, we look attractive. Hey, this is for the gentleman—how many times have you seen a beautiful woman who displayed an ugly personality that was just a great turn off? Yes, I think you understand what I am saying.

Make it a point when you look in the mirror to tell yourself that you are going to work on being a good person and display ethical and moral behavior. You will not engage in illegal activities that will bring reproach to yourself, family, friends or employer. Declare that you are a person of integrity and honor, and you have decided to live your life in a manner that provokes respect, kindness and love to others. Again, this is something that you must see as valuable attributes to display. Working on your character and personality is something that must be importance to you. No one can make you want to do it. But if you choose to work on this area, you will quickly begin to see the rewards that come with displaying positive characteristics in both your behavior and personality.

Make a list of your personal priorities.

This is a very important aspect for accepting who you are in order to become who you want to be. Although this is a challenge for most of us, it is pertinent for our success. Most of us go through life with no agenda for the day or our lives. "Whatever happens happens" is their motto. Now there is nothing wrong with not getting too serious about planning too far ahead for our lives because we do not know what is going to happen, but we should make sure that we know what is important to us and what is not. Decide what takes precedence in our lives and what should not. The reason why it is important to make a list of personal priorities is because if we do not, empty fillers will be allowed to overtake our lives, and these empty fillers are called distractions.

Too often we find ourselves getting sidetracked by distractions that get us off course in achieving our successes. Allowing these distractions to fill places in our lives is one reason many of us never achieve or discover too late the potential we have in fulfilling our purposes. Outside influences that have nothing to do with moving forward in our lives are allowed to sidetrack us and then we find ourselves behind and in a rut. Now, do not misunderstand what I am saying. I am not saying that we cannot help others or get sidetracked for a short while. This is going to happen from time to time, but unfortunately, many people allow themselves to become slaves to these outside negative distracters and end up with a lot of regrets. I am not going to help you make your personal list. This is your life, therefore your choices and your list, but I do want to assist you in making your priority list come to fruition so that you can achieve success in those areas. The following suggestions should assist you in fulfilling your personal priority list:

1. *Make the list.* Simply put, take out the time to make a list of your personal priorities. You want to write them down and when you do this, it makes the expectation become more real to you. You make an effort to become committed to it. As long as things are just rolling around in your head, you can lose the desires or talk yourself out of it. But once the list is written, it becomes a contract between you and yourself. You may even want to take it a step further and sign it. Put the date on it and sign the list. Make sure your list of priorities is concise and realistic.

2. *Be faithful to the list.* Work on your list daily if that is how you prioritized it. I don't know your goals, but it is whatever works for you. It may be something that you need to work on daily or maybe it is something that can be done on a weekly basis, but whatever your personal priority list consists of you must be faithful to it. When you are faithful to the list, it gives you a sense of accomplishment. As you begin to incorporate your list into your life, you will begin to see your fulfillment in those areas come to fruition.

3. *Discern when to put the list aside.* This is important. You must be able to discern when it is

time to allow something else to take priority over your list. This can be a difficult task especially if you are a very giving and attentive person. You also do not want to become selfish and self-centered either. An example of a good time to put the list aside, momentarily, may be to care for a sick loved one especially when there is truly no one else that can be of assistance. Another example is to take care of your own personal needs if your own health is at risk. You must determine what that is, but do not allow anything or anyone to monopolize your life and time unnecessarily.

4. *Understand that **"No"** is a good word.* If you do not remember to apply anything else I have written in this section, you must remember that "No" is a good word when it comes to sticking to your personal priority list.

   Distractions are coming; that is inevitable. There will be people who will try to pull on you and get you off your course. You cannot allow them to interfere with what you are doing. Their emergency is not your emergency. People make bad choices and want you to rescue them from the consequences of those choices. Also, there are those who will come to you because you make yourself too assessable. You will end up getting off course and it may take awhile before you can get back on track. Learn to say "No", when people want you to get involved with their bad choices.

   Often times, you will find yourself walking into a web of confusion. If you have not discerned that this is not the time to step away from your personal priority list, then say—"NO". I want to give you a formula to live by. I believe if you put it into practice, you will be just fine. Here it is—(Compassion minus wisdom equals foolishness). Simply put---compassion-wisdom=foolishness.

Work on your image.

Remember that perfecting your image plays a very vital role in your success. Let's start where you are and build on it because first things first. Rome wasn't built in a day and nor are you going to be that Sauvé and debonair person over night. It takes time, but more importantly it takes planning. You need to think about your "fashion personality" and how you can convey that in the best possible light.

Several years ago, I was an image consultant and one of the elements of the business was teaching fashion personality and color analysis. The information can be quite scientific and detailed in nature; therefore, for the sake of this book, I will just keep the information simple. Everyone has a sense of what type of fashion they want to wear, but what is your style? A very wise woman once told me that fashion is the current trend, but style is based on the individual. Sometimes based on your employment, your fashion sense may be dictated to you, but the style is what reflects who you are. For example, you may work in a bank which may require conservative attire for their conservative setting, but your style may be trendy in which you wear colors that are not so conservative---pink, yellow, green, floral prints.

The most important thing about perfecting your image is that you want to be appropriate to the setting, both work and play. People do judge you based on your attire, style and hygiene. Personally, I do not think I could do business with a bank if one of the bank tellers is wearing a see through blouse and has bright orange hair. I also do not think it would be appropriate to be on the sales floor of an exclusive retail store wearing a spike hairstyle and tattoos showing all over your body. If you want to display an image of excellence, then truly think about what you want to portray. If you do not have a lot of clothes, make sure you are neat and clean. You may not believe it, but that will make all the difference in the world. Remember what I previously said, you are trying to get there. Therefore, while you are working on your image make sure your clothing choice is not offensive and your style and hygiene are in check. Here is a cliché---Clothes may not make the man or woman, but they help.

Your image is a work in progress, so always plan on putting your best foot forward. Some people take years perfecting their images and it may even change based on your own evolution, but wearing clothes that are clean and neat and appropriate for the environment will give you a thumbs up every time.

Remember the phrase—being dead is not good for business.

This is a catchy phrase isn't it? I thought so too when I saw it and I decided to incorporate it into this chapter. "Being dead is not good for business" is important to remember because if you lose your health and sense of well-being, you will not be able to make it to work or be good for anything or anyone. It is important to understand that it takes less time to take care of yourself than it does to lose your ability to function well. Illness will come upon you from incorporating bad health habits. Recall when I shared with you about my cancer ordeal. Well, what I did not share was that I had not seen a doctor in over ten years. I had poor eating habits and did not exercise on a regular basis, plus I was under a lot of stress. Now, that was definitely a train wreck waiting to happen. Like many others, I did not concern myself with having a healthy lifestyle. As long as I did not have any aches and pains, I did not focus on my health. I was young and I looked good. I had a decent job, my son was getting ready to graduate from high school and I was dating a great guy. Life was good!

While I was on my "life high", I decided since I had not seen a doctor, I would make an appointment to have a physical. I was the picture of health when I saw the doctor and he was very impressed with me, little did I know that my life was going to drastically change; shortly after, I was diagnosed with Hodgkin's disease. I was in the fourth and last stage of the cancer. I had a tumor in my chest about 9cm and one on my spine around the same size. I went from a wheelchair to a walker and then to a cane until I was eventually able to walk on my own. Of course, I was unable to work; I was off my job for almost a year. Now I do not know if this disease was inevitable for me, or if it was a result of an unhealthy lifestyle, but surely not taking care of myself contributed to it coming to fruition.

If you are willing to take to heart what I just shared with you, then I would like to give you a few life changing tips that will help you avoid being off the job due to illness. I could have easily died from this disease; in fact, I came close to it one time. Do not take your health for granted and do not think because you do not have aches and pains right now that everything is fine. You must put into practice actions that will ensure good health and longevity. Your boss, co-workers, family and friends are depending on you to play an intricate role in their lives. If you are no longer around, it will leave a great deficit in the lives of these people. Surely, they will go on, but I am sure that they would prefer not to without you. Let's examine a few tips that might assist you in maintaining your health and a sense of well-being. I am sure that if you put them into practice, you will see and feel a significant change.

Changing your lifestyle with these helpful health tips will definitely improve your chances of occupying this earth a little bit longer.

1. *Make your bed your new best friend.* Getting plenty of rest has numerous health benefits. These are some of the benefits of a good night sleep: Better health, better sex life, less pain—(researchers have found that getting a night's sleep can supplement medication for pain), lower risk of injury, better mood, better weight control, clear thinking, better memory and a stronger immune system---(getting enough sleep can prevent the common cold).

2. *Change your eating habits---Introduce more whole foods into your diet.* We have already discussed in a previous chapter how harmful it is to have a diet primarily of bad carbohydrates, which are mainly processed foods, and then there is the danger of eating too much processed sugar. Food required for good mental and physical health include plenty of fresh fruits and vegetables and those containing essential fatty acids, for example: sardines, tuna, salmon, pumpkin and nuts. Changing your diet to more whole foods (foods that only have one ingredient) will actually help change your taste bud sensitivity. You will actually start enjoying your food and the many benefits whole foods have on your digestive system.

3. *Get moving.* Daily activities of some kind will be beneficial to health. The most natural exercise is walking. If you have a greater interest in exercise then challenge yourself by doing aerobics, weight

lifting, jogging or swimming. If you join an exercise facility, you can take advantage of all of the activities I mentioned. They even have exercises you can do sitting down. It is never too late to start doing some kind of activity to keep that blood circulating, heart rate going and muscles and joints limber. If you truly desire to maintain your health and wellness, include an exercise routine into your daily activities and see how it will enhance your life.

4. *Have regular physical checkups.* Don't just assume because there are no aches and pains that everything is alright, more than likely it is, but you want to be pro-active about your health. Start practicing a preventative regiment for your life. Have a complete annual physical, mammograms and pap smears if you are a woman and other preventative screening tests that are given to both sexes. An ounce of prevention is worth a pound of cure. Remember it is far easier to maintain good health than to take care of an illness once it comes upon you. Having a physical only takes a short span of time from your day. It can prevent an insidious disease from starting and ensure that you have a more enjoyable and fulfilled life.

5. *Get a hobby and join social groups.* Outside activities that involve meeting new people is always good. Being around the same people at work can cause you to become stagnated and bored. It may also decrease your social growth. Get involved by joining groups that help develop you as a person. For example if you like photography, join a photography group. If your interest is reading, you may want to join a book club. Maybe becoming more active in your local church will jolt your life. Whatever you may have an interest in;

pursue joining a group and meet new people. If you have a more introverted personality, then maybe you may want to spend time with an individual that you enjoy and the two of you can participate in activities together. The bottom line is this; do something that sparks your interest and helps you grow socially and intellectually.

Adapting to a healthy lifestyle is what we all should aim towards accomplishing. If you desire to be at your best at all times, then begin by doing what I suggested. Of course, there are many more tips I can give to you, the five that I mentioned will be a great start to begin your health and wellness journey. You want to be effective and productive in every area of your life, especially the workplace. You bring value to the job and your boss appreciates your input into the productivity of his business. If you are ill and cannot come to work to be productive, not only does it impact your workplace, but it also impacts others around you. Work on staying healthy. Your good health is more valuable than precious jewels. You only have one life; cherish it, and remember the phrase----"being dead is NOT good for business."

Chapter Six

Key # 6: Treat Others with Honor and Respect

Treating others with honor and respect is one of the greatest golden rules for our personal lives as well as in the workplace. Needless to say though, it is often the one rule that is the most abused. If you want to experience fulfillment and success in every area of your life, you must adhere to this principle. Everyone is familiar with the motto—treat others as you want to be treated. Experiencing fulfillment in every area of our lives starts with how we see ourselves and how we interact with other people. I stated how we see ourselves as a factor for fulfillment because in order to honor and respect others, we must first set the example for others through how we honor and respect ourselves.

Enough has been said in the previous chapters as to how we must focus on being our best, now you want to transcend that focus to other people you come in contact with. If you truly learned from the previous chapters about self-love, self-respect, self-image and self-fulfillment, then you are ready to act on what you have learned by honoring and respecting other people on and off the job. There are several areas that I would like to expound upon that are the most prevalent to honoring and respecting others. If you work on these areas, you will begin to experience a less stressful and burdensome environment, and a more peaceful and fulfilled life.

Stop and avoid gossiping.

Gossiping is one of the most malicious and deadliest forms of abuse you can render and/or experience. It will literally destroy your soul. ***Proverbs 10: 14*** in the Contemporary English Version says, ***"If you have good sense, you will learn all you can, but foolish talk will soon destroy you"***. Through gossip, marriages and friendships have been destroyed. People have lost their jobs and business opportunities have been missed out because of gossip. I do not think that the average person realizes just how much damage gossip causes. When you get involved with gossip, you have strayed far away from honoring and respecting anyone and this also includes yourself. Gossip is a form of deceit and it puts a spotlight on the lack of integrity that one has in his or her character.

If it is your desire to excel in your personal life as well as in the workplace, stop and avoid getting involved in gossip. You want to be a person that your friends and fellow employees can trust and depend on. You do not want people watching their backs when you are around. If you want to gain true friends and get that promotion on your job, then gossip cannot be a part of your daily activity in your life. I know you know people who engage in gossip and although you may not have a problem when someone else is the topic of discussion, rest assure you will be on the list one day to be spotlighted. Remember to treat people the way you want to be treated.

Be mindful of how you treat and speak to people.

If you truly want to respect and honor others, then start by controlling your actions towards people and what comes out of your mouth. I hear so many horror stories of how people are being mentally and verbally abused on their jobs. There have been cases that have often led to people taking sick leaves because of stress. Who wants to spend the first eight hours of their day being abused? The workplace is a place of business where its primary focus is to perform a service and/or sell a product. People are necessary to be in those positions to fulfill those tasks. Employers cannot afford to have people staying home because of stress and physical ailment as a result of harassment and bullying in the workplace. Now most of you may think that the harshness comes from the boss alone, but there are many noted incidences where fellow co-workers are the culprits.

Having respect and honor for others by controlling your actions and what you say to people will go a long way. Not only will you excel in your personal life, but acting accordingly will bring forth opportunities on your job too. By speaking with respect and honor to people, you will have a greater influence on your work performance as well as your interaction with others. The work environment will be pleasant and productivity will increase. A team effort will come into play, therefore igniting a sense of cohesiveness. My motto is this---“when I leave my home for the first eight hours of my day, I want to enjoy them”. Make that your motto too. Be kind, and again, treat others the way you want to be treated. Be mindful of how you treat and speak to people. When you master this---it will take you a long way.

Be helpful as much as possible.

As I mentioned in the previous paragraph, working as a team gets more accomplished. Giving a fellow co-worker assistance shows good workmanship as well as getting kudos for your character. It lets your employer know that you are not out to showboat and that you are concerned about the success of the company. If there is a deadline and a fellow co-worker falls behind or they have an overload, assist where you can. Maybe even give an additional training to someone who does not quite understand the task at hand. I am sure your boss will appreciate the initiative you take to assure that your co-worker is working efficiently.

It takes a person of character to think of others and not be self-absorbed. If you are working on getting a promotion or desiring to be selected to plan the family's reunion, remember others are not just looking for someone who can spearhead it, but they also want to choose someone who is a team player and who cares. Looking out for others is one true sign of a leader, because a leader is going to help bring out the best in each person on their team. Therefore, being helpful and assisting others to complete a task shows that you are willing to make sacrifices when needed, but also you should know when not to over extend yourself. The objective is to get as much done as possible.

Remember, you can catch more flies with honey.

This is a saying my mother use to always tell me. Although it is scientifically true, this saying also holds true to getting a positive reaction we want from people. For every action, there is a positive or negative reaction; which reaction do you want to experience in your life when you interact with your family, friends, and co-workers. The choice is yours. If we show respect and honor, more than likely we are going to get a positive reaction. I have not met a person yet who does not respond well to positive stimuli—a kind word, or a positive gesture. Even when you have to give someone constructive criticism if you tell them how wonderful they are first, they will be able to handle the constructive criticism later. It takes just as much effort to give a cruel word as it does a kind one; either way, you have to think about the words coming out of your mouth.

If you truly want to take control of your life from the inside out and find fulfillment in every area of your life, then work on developing better interpersonal skills. That is the key word—skills. It is a skill treating people with respect and honor; it takes discipline. It is so easy to treat people on the basis of how we feel. You are not a "Lone Ranger" and success is not going to come to you without a "hand up" from other people, contrary to what you may believe. In other words, we need each other to accomplish our goals and be our best on and off the job. If you operate with self-constraint, discipline, and kindness, you will find that these qualities will afford you many doors of positive opportunities.

Chapter Seven

Key #7: Dare to be Happy and Learn to be Content

It is a fact that people who love what they do are highly motivated people, and are usually happy and content people overall. Now aren't you the least bit curious as to how these people achieved this feat? Well, in this chapter, we are going to embark on a journey that will open the door to happiness and contentment by following just a few of the suggestions that I will share with you. Many of these suggestions are not new to you, but sometimes we just need someone to give us a strong nudge over and over again until that light bulb goes off and we get it. By no means do I want you to think that happy and content people are lackadaisical people without a care in the world. Oh no, that is far from the truth. People who are happy and content with their lives are high achievers and are disciplined people. They have learned the art of distressing and not sweating the small stuff.

Happiness and contentment are spiritual endorphins that allow us to experience joy and peace in a not so joyous and peaceful world. When we make a decision to be happy and content, we take back our control. We become the navigator of our destiny as we choose to walk in our purpose. Studies have been done that show that people who are happy and love what they do are highly motivated by their own enthusiasm to continually better themselves and improve their performance. They are good listeners and have a sharp learning curve. In addition, they are highly creative, charismatic, interpersonal and good team players. Now I don't know about you Mr. Boss, but that sounds like a person I would want to work for my company. Hopefully, what I described is what I can encourage everyone reading this book to achieve---achieve being happy. Whatever is ailing you, let it go. Put your reservations to the side and allow me to share with you some suggestions for achieving happiness and contentment in the next few paragraphs.

Stop chasing the dollar and pursue your purpose.

Stop chasing the dollar and pursue your purpose is what I had to learn after surviving an insidious disease. As I mentioned, previously, I was diagnosed with Hodgkin's disease and I was in the fourth and last stage of the disease. Before the diagnoses, my only goal was to make a lot of money. I worked like a work horse day and night, literally, and the only thing important to me was how I could make more money. I was so "money driven" that when I was diagnosed with cancer, I told my doctor to give me my treatment so that I could go back to working my daily twelve hour schedule. He laughed and told me that I would not be going back to work for a while. I laughed back at him and told him—"watch me". Well, he was right. I did not see my job for almost nine months and I must tell you that that time off gave me a new perspective about my life, my purpose and working a job.

I know that most people work to achieve and maintain a certain lifestyle, whether it is a big house in the suburbs or a fine luxury vehicle. Some people just find it comforting to have a lot of money put away for that rainy day they are anticipating coming someday. Others want money so they can buy whatever they want to buy and go on exotic luxurious vacations. Then you have those who want a lot of money just so they can pay off their current bills and create new ones. Really, there is nothing wrong with any of those reasons if this is what suits you. Whatever reason people choose to work is their business; people are going to do what they want to do. But I had to do some soul searching during my illness, and I realized that I personally had the whole thing backwards. I learned that money should be the reward not the thing being pursued.

When we make earning money as our primary aim to go to work, we lose a sense of direction for our lives and the reason why we go to work. Although working is a good thing, not all work is good for the people who hold those positions. Come on, you know what I mean. How many times have you called a business and the person who answers the phone is rude to you, or even worse, they do not have any information about what you are inquiring about. You know it is just a means to an end with this person---it's just a J O B. They have poor communication and interpersonal skills; heck, you found that out when they didn't even bother to say, "Hello". Yet, someone hired them to be the first person you speak to when you call their business. Here is another scenario—a person always showing up for work late and paying more attention to the clock than his or her job performance. They take long lunch breaks when they can get away with it, and their co-workers hate working with them. They just bring down the morale of the workplace and that certainly is not good for business.

The pursuit of money alone hinders you from enjoying your personal lives because most of your time is spent on regretting going back to the workplace, or you tell yourself you do not have time for anything else. You can't make time for family, friends or just having a great time on a much needed break. You feel despondent and depressed. You lack ambition and drive. You find yourself indulging in things you know is not you, such as overeating and smoking cigarettes. In your opinion, life has become a drag. I can go on and on, but I believe you get my drift.

Well, you ask yourself, how do I get out of this rut? The solution is not easy, but it is possible. It starts from understanding the purpose of work and why all of mankind has been ordained to do it. The concept of working was created to give mankind a sense of worth or better said, to add value to his or her life. When we leave our homes to go into the workplace, it should be to pursue value for our lives. Work helps us realize who we are in terms of our abilities, talents and skills. Through these actions, we often discover just what our life purpose is that should be fulfilled. It is that thing that we have a passion to do and would initially be willing to work absolutely free to do it.

Several years ago, I read the testimony of the famous motivational speaker, Les Brown, when he shared in one of his books that he started speaking free because he loved it so much. He knew he had something to give to the world through his speaking; a message that would motivate others to achieve their goals and be fulfilled. He had jobs that helped him discover that he truly had the gift of "gab" and he knew he wanted to do more. He eventually stepped out in faith to pursue what he knew he was capable of doing, because he loved it so much; now Les Brown is a multimillionaire. He will never have to speak free again, but he may do it just because he is not chasing the dollar---he pursued his purpose and he realizes that the money was the reward. I understand that everyone is not called to be a motivational speaker and I am not implying that you have to have your own business to be happy. I am simply saying that through the action of working, you add value to your life and when your mindset is that of adding value to you through work, your paycheck will be looked upon in the manner in which it was intended---the reward.

Change your mindset and stop applying for jobs that are going to give you a paycheck. Apply for a job that is going to give value to your life. If you love to sell, pursue a job in sales, don't apply for a receptionist job. If you love working with your hands, don't apply for a job in sales just because someone told you there's money in sales. That may not be where the money is for you. If you love to work with fashion, go into fashion retail. It can lead you to becoming a buyer and maybe owning your own store; don't apply for a job in the factory making cars and be miserable. You may be on a dead end job, and you may feel trapped. I promise you, you are not.

Begin to visualize your change, and every opportunity you have, start pursuing what your interests are. If you do not know what your interests are, do a self assessment. There is something that you enjoy doing and it may even be a passion, but you many not think you can make money doing it. Again, I promise you—if you can see yourself doing it; it can bring a monetary reward. I often think about the playwright and screen writer, Tyler Perry, who has written numerous plays and movie scripts. When he started out, he lived out of his car and didn't have a lot of help. He always wanted to write plays and money was probably not his motivation for writing them. Yes, he needed to eat and take care of himself, but his desire and passion to see his work on stage is what drove him to continue striving. You know the rest of the story. I believe he is now a billionaire. His financial reward probably exceeded his expectations, but the pursuit of purpose is what brought everything to fruition. Now everyone is not called to be a playwright or screenwriter, but we are all called to pursue our purpose and walk in it.

Slow down and enjoy the simple things in life.

Slow down and enjoy the simple things in life because tomorrow is not promised to any of us. I often hear so many stories of people working all their adult lives striving for the moment of retirement and shortly afterwards they die; what a tragedy. If we could examine their lives, we would discover that all they did was work, work, work, and work some more. The children would grow up and they could not even remember one of their birthday parties, the couples never having an opportunity to spend that much time with each other because of the work schedule, and sadly, they never took out time to do any of the things they desired to do. Everything was put off for retirement.

Does that sound like anyone you know or does that sound like you? Enjoy the sunset or admire a rainbow after a rainy day, or even just appreciate the breeze that flows across your face. These are a few of the simple things that make life enjoyable. When was the last time you saw a good movie or took a trip just for the weekend; driving on the open road? Many of you are saying I don't have time. I have to work overtime just to meet the demand of the household expenses. Excuses, excuses, excuses that is always what I hear; one day you are going to wake up and wished you had done something with your time besides work. It doesn't have to be that way though. You can make up in your mind that you are going to dare to be happy and content by enjoying those little things that you take for granted and purposely plan events that will put a smile on your face.

After my cancer ordeal, I made up my mind that I was going to stop chasing the dollar and begin to really start pursuing my purpose and enjoying some of the wonderful things God created for me. One of the things I did was take a trip with one of my good friends and my dog. We visited a friend who lived in Bangor, Michigan which is near Lake Michigan. I enjoyed it thoroughly. There was a lot of farm area where people grew their own fruit such as strawberries. In fact, the very first time I ate a gala apples was at one of the local markets. I have been hooked on those apples ever since. The highlight of the trip was going walking on the shores of Lake Michigan. The air was so clean and refreshing. It was like I was born again. My mind was clear from any concerns and my body felt a renewal. I was with my good friend and my little girl, Daphne (my dog) and I was the happiest I had ever been. Nothing mattered to me; I felt free and alive! Another year, we had the opportunity to visit the Sleeping Bear Dunes near Traverse City. Again, it was a wonderful time just enjoying nature. Seeing the sun set near Lake Michigan is a view that you must see. It was like being in the presence of God.

It is a choice to dare to be happy, and slowing down to enjoy the simple things in life will have to be something that you make a priority. It is not going to happen by itself. The sun in always going to rise and set, but no one can make you watch it. Lake Michigan will always be there, but no one can make you walk on its shores and appreciate its splendor. Taking a weekend trip or getting in your car to drive along a scenic route will always be options, but no one can make you do them. Enjoying the simple things and choosing to be happy is within your reach. Okay, maybe you can't take a trip or be around to see the sunrise or set, but what about spending time with your family. Go see a movie, take a ride through a neighborhood where you can daydream about your dream house. Go to the park with your kids, or find a project that you can do with your children like wash the car and purposely get them wet; make it fun. Don't make life so serious. While you are pursuing your purpose, enjoy the ride. Its okay to take the scenic route of life. There are a lot of wonderful things to see and enjoy along the way.

Don't Sweat the Small Stuff, It's all small stuff.

"Don't sweat the small stuff; it's all small stuff" should be your motto to living a stress free life. If you keep this motto ever before you, you will be well on your way to enjoying happiness. Happiness is based on circumstances and situations and oftentimes, we are the ones who are responsible for those circumstances and situations we experience in life. My grandmother use to say that most of the problems we have in life we bring them on ourselves; I mentioned that statement earlier in the book. Letting go of past hurts, staying out of toxic relationships, watching your diet, and getting enough rest. These are all factors that contribute to whether or not we are going to have a stress free life or should I say have as less stress as possible. We are never going to avoid all stress. It comes with life; in fact, some forms of stress is good because it gives us that added push and drive that we need to accomplish our goals. But having stress that warrants illness, addictions, and even leading to death is not good.

Most people worry if they do not have anything to worry about. Everything can be going fine in their lives and they worry about that. They think that because nothing is wrong, something bad is about to happen. Instead of just enjoying life and realizing that life may just be giving you a break or maybe you just made good choices that warranted good things to happen for you---you want to put an omen in the mix and mess everything up. This is also true in the workplace—the job brings enough stress to itself. Don't worry about a promotion that's six months away. Don't compare yourself to that girl who is wearing those sexy clothes to get the boss' attention. You want your promotion and pay raise to be based upon your job performance and work ethics. Stop allowing others to bully you just because they have more seniority. There are laws to protect you from that behavior. Remember that life is what you make it and if you allow the small stuff to use up your entire arsenal, when the big problems finally come, you will be out of ammunition.

Before I was diagnosed with cancer, I use to concern myself with a lot of unnecessary matters. I would just lie around and think about things to worry about. I had to soon teach myself to just start removing unimportant matters from my plate. Even if it was a matter I had to confront, I did not confront it until I had to. I have since learned to give myself mini goals to complete each day and be content with that. The same applies on the job. You only have so many hours in the work day to complete certain tasks. Prioritize and do what is most important for that day and be efficient. Your boss would much rather you complete five things out of eight, correctly, than to complete all eight task with mistakes. Take a deep breath and take your time; work diligently and efficiently. You will not stress yourself out, and you and your boss will be satisfied.

Although I am retired from my job at Detroit Public schools, I still practice this. I try not to concern myself with a matter that is not on my plate today; I deal with it when it is time. I still set mini goals to complete each day and I feel great when I efficiently complete them. I have also learned to relieve stress by walking my dog (which by the way is a great walking partner), by reading, writing and also praying. I personally do not want to leave here prematurely. It is my desire that everyone reading this book makes it their goal to live a healthy and long life. In order to achieve this goal, you must learn that life is like a play, you are only responsible for your own part.

Get up every morning thanking God for it. Be grateful for everything you possess—health, money, material possessions, etc, and know that each day is given to you so that you can dare to be happy and content in this life. You only have one life. You don't get an opportunity to do it again. Stop chasing the dollar and start pursing your purpose, make it your business to purposely start enjoying the simple things in life and finally, don't sweat the small stuff, it's all small stuff. You're in charge of your choices. Dare to be happy and content in your personal life as well as on your job. You'll be glad you did.

Chapter Eight

Key # 8: Put God First and Trust Him with Your Future

Most successful and driven people have some kind of spiritual connection. For the most part, many successful people have come to realize that they cannot be fulfilled in any area of their lives without acknowledging a higher being. It is almost impossible to exist without some form of spirituality and relationship with your Creator. Again, the motivational speaker, Les Brown often makes reference to God and his success. In fact, many great businessmen tell how their connection with God catapulted their success. The late Dr. Myles Monroe has written numerous books and spoken to fortune 500 companies about the importance of having a relationship with God if they truly wanted to maximize their potential and bring their company to that apex of success. Dr. Monroe taught them that it is good to acknowledging that God is trustworthy of their future plans. There have also been numerous studies done that revealed that people who are in constant communication with God have less stress and better coping skills. They are in better health and have fulfilled lasting relationships. All of these factors contribute to the success in your professional lives and jobs.

This chapter is very important because it puts the icing on the cake so to speak. If you have read this book in its entirety, then you must realize that fulfillment is not something that you can achieve alone, there must be some divine intervention. Putting God first and trusting God with your future is not a suggestion, it is a mandate. I often tell my son, who is a great business man; there are three keys to obtain and maintain success. Put God first and trust Him with your future, make good choices and avoid toxic relationships. If he continues to do the first, the other two will be fulfilled. In this book, we have already thoroughly discussed the last two keys. Now in this chapter, I would like to discuss the first key I gave to my son. Of course, I cannot make anyone do this, in fact, some of you who have gotten this far in the book many decide that this is where you're going to put the book down, and I assure you that you will be doing yourself a great disservice if you do.

Personally, I do not understand how people can exist in this world without having an ally that they know have their backs. Who would better know what is best for you than the one who created you? Who has given you your abilities, gifts and talents? Therefore, who would best know how you should put these qualities to use? It is to your benefit to understand that you have a divine purpose and it is vast in nature. You have an assignment to contribute substance to the world be it as a sales person, an attorney, a fireman, a farmer, or whatever. It all comes together to serve the better good for mankind.

Life is like a puzzle and we are all a piece of it. When it is put together, is shows the big picture. There is a plan for the world and God wants you to fulfill your part. When you begin to see your value (purpose for working), you will want to acknowledge your Creator in order to understand just what part you play in completing the master plan. There is truly a divine plan and a purpose for our lives, but we must remember that it is already mapped out. We do not have to concern ourselves with the outcome as long as we acknowledge our Creator and give Him full reign in our lives and trust Him with it. The following principles will help you put God first and trust Him with your future:

- **Give God the first part of your day**. Start your day off with God through prayer, meditation, reading spiritual books, etc. Having a God focus will help you develop a relationship with Him and will allow you to build trust. You cannot trust someone you do not spend time with or know. God is no different than developing a relationship with a human being. You must put some time and effort into it.

- **Acknowledge God in every daily activity**. Once you have learned to communicate and build a trust with God, begin to acknowledge Him in every daily activity, such as work, investments, relationships, etc. You can begin to give Him the assignment of taking care of all of your affairs. Remember, He desires for you to succeed. Don't make any major decisions without acknowledging Him first. It's like letting a certified mechanic examine a used car before you buy it. You will not go wrong if you check in with the expert. He is knowledgeable about everything, especially what's best for your life.

- **Be assured that He is leading and guiding you**. When you have given Him the assignment of taking care of your affairs and you trust Him with it, sit back and relax. Know that the outcome is going to be great. He wants you to fulfill your destiny and live a prosperous, long and fulfilled life. Anything short of that is not His perfect will for you. Remember, it is not your plan that is going to be fulfilled, it is His plan. He has just given you a portion to complete it.

> Even when you feel discouraged, He is still carrying out the plan. You may sit down on the job, but God doesn't. You can rest assured that God is not caught off guard. There are no opps when He is in the plan. He is leading you and guiding you when you acknowledge that this is His job in your life.

Lasting happiness isn't found in money alone or a career success, but that does not mean these things are wrong. God wants us to have these things; in fact, He created them to be enjoyed. Also understand that when you put God first and trust Him with your future, He will actually give you these things. But you must never let anything God gives you rob Him of first place in your life. I would like to share a scripture that sums up all that I have said.

"Happy is the man who delights in doing his commands. His children shall be honored everywhere, for good men's sons have a special heritage. He himself shall be wealthy, and his good deeds will never be forgotten. When darkness overtakes him, light will come bursting in. He is kind and merciful—and all goes well for the generous man who conducts his business fairly. Such a man will not be overthrown by evil circumstances. God's constant care of him will make a deep impression on all who see it. He does not fear bad news, nor live in dread of what may happen; for he is settled in his mind that God will take care of him. That is why he is not afraid, but can calmly face his enemies. He gives generously to those in need. His deeds will never be forgotten. He shall influence and honor." (Psalms 112:1-9, NIV).

Now that we have covered the areas that greatly impact our lives---relationships, emotional stability, finances, health and wellness, and our relationship with God, we can begin to see how these areas impact everything about us, including our jobs and its performance. It is your choice to discover how affective the information can help you realize and maximize your potential by walking in your purpose.

Your job is what adds value to your life, but not without the other components being on point. If you truly want to take control of your life from the inside out, then think seriously about putting these eight effective keys to work in your life. All of them are important to the other. Don't leave any of them out because they all will help bring fulfillment to your life. You have all heard the cliché, "You can lead a horse to water, but you cannot make him drink it". Think about it, why would you have to force a horse to drink if his body is longing for water from being thirsty? It is no different with this book presenting eight keys to help you realize that fulfillment is possible if you apply what you have learned to your life and continue to practice it. I had to learn these keys and apply them to my life in order to reach a sense of fulfillment. I understand what it is like to be stuck in a rut not having a sense of direction, feeling helpless and hopeless. A job is not the answer to all of your concerns, and it certainly won't be if you have other issues that outweigh what is going on with your job.

It is time to take a stand and think about every area of your life and understand that it must be in sync with your professional goals. One cannot be truly successful without the other. Oh yes, we see people who seemingly appear successful, but if we truly take a closer look, we will see a broken and contrite person. Who wants to live like that? Do you? Let's make up our minds to do it right and fulfill the plan that our Creator has for us to complete on the Earth. We do not have time to waste.

Fulfillment comes from making a choice to change the things that keep us bound and weary; thus not living our best life now. Continually, procrastination places us in a continuous rut and in stagnation, but our onward drive gives us the ability to complete our life's task and experience all the things we are destined to experience that is good for us. Don't wait until you have hit rock bottom to get up and do something. Do it now. Take control of your life from the inside out and use the eight keys that I have given you to experience fulfillment on your job and every area of your life.

Conclusion

Taking control of your life from the inside out is not a suggestion, it is a mandate that we all should adhere too. If we are going to live prosperous and fulfilled lives, we have to maintain a lifestyle that will warrants its fruition. For the most part, people do not want to live self-destructive lives. They want to live a long life and enjoy the splendors that this world has to offer, but often times because of unforeseen interruptions, that desire is delayed or never realized. There are opportunities given to everyone to realize and fulfill their dreams if they are willing to put in the work. Yes, you must be willing to put in the work. Like anything worth having, you must work at it and wait to see the fruit of your labor. Unfortunately, we live in a society where most people have a microwave mentality. They want it fast whether it's authentic or not. "***Taking Control of Your Life from the Inside Out—Eight Keys to Fulfillment on Your Job and Every Area of Your Life***" will help you reexamine and redirect your priorities and challenge you to step out into uncharted territory if you desire to realize all that lies within you. This book was written to challenge you to realize potential and rid yourself of the barriers that hinder growth, and success in every area of your life. Whether it is in your personal relationships or changing your eating habits to start feeling good about yourself, you must begin changing your life by taking the first step by applying these principles.

Making a decision to come out of toxic relationships will afford you the luxury to finally give your heart a rest—literally. You can add several more years to your life span when you make the choice to get rid of the weasels in your life. When you have chosen to only allow yourself to be around people who celebrate and love you, you will have the strength to forgive those who hurt you and forgive yourself and the situation. You will no longer have to allow the pain to hover over you. When you have realized that you no longer have to be subjected to pain, you will begin to work on altering the areas that hindered you from progressing such as past failures, poor choices and procrastination. You can now tap into the areas that help you realize and release your potential, but in order to achieve this, you must work on getting rid of bad habits and rituals. Bad habits are created by a pattern of behavior that takes place over time. The same is true when you want to create a good habit or ritual. If we are going to achieve success, then we must eliminate the forces that weaken the odds.

We all look in the mirror and we are often our worst critics, but we also can be our best makeover artists too. When we realize that we are not perfect, we can strive to be the one that gives ourselves leverage to start right where we are. No pretences will be allowed—just the pure unadulterated truth—what you see is what you get. That is where we should all start if we are going to go from that caterpillar to that beautiful butterfly or that ugly duckling to that beautiful swan. Self-acceptance of who we are, presently, will help us become the best person we were intended to be.

Having worked on improving ourselves will also challenge us to properly interact with others, be it our co-workers, family or friends or mere acquaintances. If we are going to genuinely learn to appreciate fulfillment on this earth, then we must realize honor and respect is a major factor in our interaction with others. True success is not achieved by mistreatment and self absorbed agendas, but it is achieved when we realize that it serves as a catalyst to serve others. Treating the people around you with honor and respect will open the door for many great opportunities and blessings. Because you would not have violated the spiritual and natural law of reciprocity, you will not have to concern yourself with negative karma coming upon you.

Having healthy and fulfilled relationships help complete our objective for achieving happiness and contentment in our lives. When we have incorporated positive behavior with others, we are well on our way to achieving harmony in our world, but let's take it one step further. Even when we are not around others, we should strive to have happiness and contentment in our lives at all times.

Now although this may be a challenge for many of you, dare to make it your business that you are going to be happy and content. Appreciate the simple things in life; the cool breeze blowing across your face and the birds singing early in the morning. When was the last time you even thought about appreciating those things? Challenging yourself to find something to be grateful for everyday and consciously seeking it will assist you in fulfilling your quest for happiness and contentment one day at a time. It is a great de-stressor and when you can achieve going through life without carrying the cares of this world, you are just that much closer to realizing that you can achieve fulfillment.

When everything is all said and done, the final chapter that sums it all up is realizing that you cannot do it alone. Looking up—just like Kutta Kente did in the biographical saga, "Roots.", He held his newborn baby girl up in his out stretched arms to the sky and said, "Behold, the one person that is greater than you". When we come to realize that success is not success unless the one person greater than us holds the reigns, we will never fully reach our destiny. Work was created and ordained by God to bring value to our lives. He is the one who gives us our work assignments. Like building a house from the ground up, it takes different people with different skills to complete the building of the house. No skilled man is less or more important than the other. They have the blueprint, but it all comes together because the architect had a plan.

God is the architect of our lives and He has a plan for us. We all have been given abilities, talents and skills, but we must now learn to utilize them to complete the plan that was mandated for our lives. First, every area of our lives must be in sync if we are going to truly achieve success. If it is not in sync with God's plan, then we must take control of it by bringing it into balance. Through applying these principles that will bring about change, we can then fulfill His plan and walk in our destinies that God has preordained for us.

I have outlined eight keys to bring fulfillment to your life, and they work when they are systematically and earnestly applied to the areas suggested. Yes, it is possible to have fulfillment on your job and every area of your life by applying the principles in this book. This may not be new information to many of you, but it is needed information for all of you.

Take the first step to changing your life and experience fulfillment on your job and every area of your life. Take charge and desire to be the best you can be in your professional and personal lives. Stop chasing the dollar and pursue purpose and understand the value of work and your value to your employer and yourself. Wake up each day with a new agenda—giving your best to yourself and the world around you. Come on, you can do it. Take control of your life from the inside out, and apply the eight keys that will bring fulfillment on your job and every area of your life.

"I say this because I know the plans that I have for you." This message is from God. "I have good plans for you. I don't plan to hurt you. I plan to give you hope and a good future", (Jeremiah 29: 11, ERV).

ABOUT THE AUTHOR

Tunishai Ford is an enthusiastic motivational speaker, empowerment trainer and educator. She is the founder and CEO of *Your Own Uniqueness, Inc.*, a non-profit (501c3) which deals with self-improvement and overcoming barriers that hinder individuals from reaching their full potential and walking in their destiny. She has experience in the business arena in the area of empowerment and personal achievement workshops and seminars. Her expertise has allotted her the opportunity to do educational classes for Detroit public schools teaching employability skills and life skill classes, and motivational speeches for graduating students from vocational classes. Dr. Ford has also done workshops for the City of Detroit, and Monroe bank and Trust. She has received numerous certificates and awards for her life work in the community and in business, such as the ***Testimony of Resolution Award*** from the City of Detroit, and ***Woman of the Year Award*** from the National Association of Professional Women(NAPW)—2010/2011.

To learn more about Dr. Ford, please visit her website at www.drtford.com to find out about her workshops, seminars and other services. Also check out her other books.

Other books by Dr. Tunishai Anne Ford

This is a Comma in Your Life,
NOT a Period

I Miss the Hugs,
But NOT the Hurts

The Spirit in You

Order them today on
www.drtford.com

To contact
Dr. Tunishai Anne Ford for workshops
or other speaking engagements,
please email her at you.inc@hotmail.com.

For more information about her products and
services, visit her site at www.drtford.com.